SOMETIMES I'M ANXIOUS

Sky Pony Press books may be purchased in bulk at special discounts for sales promotion, corporate gifts, fund-raising, or educational purposes. Special editions can also be created to specifications. For details, contact the Special Sales Department, Sky Pony Press, 307 West 36th Street, 11th Floor, New York, NY 10018 or info@skyhorsepublishing.com.

Sky Pony® is a registered trademark of Skyhorse Publishing, Inc.®, a Delaware corporation.

Visit our website at www.skyponypress.com.

10 9

Manufactured in China, January 2024
This product conforms to CPSIA 2008

Library of Congress Cataloging-in-Publication Data is available on file.

Text by Poppy O'Neill
Interior and cover design by Summersdale Publishers Ltd.

Print ISBN: 978-1-5107-4748-7

Printed in China

SOMETIMES I'M ANXIOUS

A Child's Guide to Overcoming Anxiety

Poppy O'Neill

Foreword by Amanda Ashman-Wymbs

Sky Pony Press
New York

CONTENTS

FOREWORD

Amanda Ashman-Wymbs, Counsellor and Psychotherapist, registered and accredited by the British Association for Counselling and Psychotherapy

Having raised two girls and after working in the public and private sector with many young people therapeutically for over ten years, it is clear to me that issues of anxiety are prevalent in our children and our society today. Understanding the symptoms and causes, and knowing where to go and what to do with these feelings and behaviors, can be an overwhelming and confusing experience for both the child and the parents.

Poppy O'Neill's *Sometimes I'm Anxious* is a simple and fun workbook for children to use independently or with the support of their parents or carers. It sets out explanations and examples of anxious feelings, thoughts and experiences in a clear format and shows the child how to understand and overcome these in manageable ways. I particularly like how the book is infused with big positive statements, which will make an impression on the child's mind, and examples of how other children have dealt with anxiety, as so often young people can feel that they are the only ones experiencing these fears and knowing that is not the case can be hugely comforting.

As anxiety-based feelings and thoughts are usually about something that *might* happen in the future, having the introduction to mindfulness is also invaluable in learning to manage and transcend symptoms—the more that children can connect to the reality of their present experience through their breath, body and senses, the more they will naturally learn to feel calm and happy again.

This is a much-needed and great self-help book to support children when they are experiencing difficult times.

INTRODUCTION: A GUIDE FOR PARENTS AND CARERS

How to use this book

Sometimes I'm Anxious is a practical guide to anxiety for children. Using cognitive behavioral therapy techniques developed by child psychologists, the simple activities and encouraging text will help your child to overcome anxious thoughts and feelings.

Anxiety is an evolutionary phenomenon that stems back to the dawn of mankind, to a time when remaining hypervigilant to potential threats often meant the difference between life and being eaten by a sabre-toothed tiger for our cave-dwelling ancestors. For modern humans, anxiety can still help us make sensible decisions and avoid dangerous situations. While occasional anxious feelings are common, it becomes a problem when anxiety starts to get in the way of leading a normal life.

We all have worries—big ones and small ones—and your child might seem to be more prone to worrying or phobias than others their age. Sometimes no matter how much you reassure them, certain things can prey on their minds. The thing about anxiety is, it doesn't follow logic: anxiety can take the form of realistic or unrealistic worries, and it can be very difficult for children to explain or shake off.

You might remember separation anxiety from the toddler years—younger children can get tearful and clingy when leaving their parent or carer. While separation anxiety is a normal and healthy developmental phase, anxiety can manifest itself in a variety of ways. Sometimes anxiety can be persistent beyond just a phase, and can cause the child undue distress.

This book is aimed at children aged 8 to 12, an age when it can feel like there's a lot to worry about. Exams, friendship woes, changes to their bodies, a greater interest in their physical attractiveness and that of others are all new and sometimes daunting experiences. Children this age might start using social media, and their awareness of the news, popular media and the world as a whole is developing. It's no wonder this can be an anxious time.

Signs of anxiety

Looking out for these signs can help determine if anxiety is a problem for your child. They may exhibit these signs most of the time, or only in certain situations:

- They are reluctant to try new things

- They seem unable to cope with everyday challenges

- They find it hard to concentrate

- They have trouble sleeping or eating properly

- They are prone to angry outbursts

- They experience intrusive, unwanted thoughts that they struggle to get out of their head

- They worry excessively that bad things are going to happen

- They avoid everyday activities such as going to school, seeing friends or going out in public

- They seek constant reassurance

Keep a note when you notice any of these behaviors. Where were they? What had happened just before, or was about to happen? This way you can work out if there is a particular situation that is causing your child to feel anxious.

Remember, anxieties can be difficult for children to talk about, but it's never too late to start helping them conquer their worries.

Talking it over

When a child is suffering with anxiety, it's tempting to shield them from the thing they're worried about. Your instinct might be to say: "if you're worried about the party, don't go." But the message your child receives is that their feelings of anxiety mean they aren't capable of doing the things they find challenging.

It's important to talk things through with your child, exploring potential situations in a calm way, to really get to the heart of their worries. Focus on solutions and realistic outcomes rather than all the things that could go wrong. Offer your support and let them know you will take them seriously and work with them to solve the problem. It's essential that children learn how to effectively deal with negative thoughts and feelings in order to become independent, self-assured young people.

Getting started

Guide your child through the chapters and activities in this book—just one at a time, perhaps once a week or every few days. Allow your child to set the pace and work on the activities independently—this is important because by developing your child's independence you are showing them that they are able to have a go at challenges by themselves. The activities are designed to get them thinking about themselves and how they deal with worries while giving them the tools needed to recognize and overcome anxiety. When your child feels calm and capable they are better equipped to deal with the challenges of everyday life. Make sure they know that they have your support and that you will take their worries seriously, even if they seem trivial to you. Help them learn new habits to deal with their problems independently, then watch their confidence grow.

This book aims to help you and your child understand and tackle anxious thoughts and feelings. However, if you have any serious concerns about your child's mental health, beyond what is covered in this book, your pediatrician or family doctor is the best person to turn to for further advice.

HOW TO USE THIS BOOK: A GUIDE FOR CHILDREN

This book is for you if you often...

- ✿ Feel nervous, worried or afraid

- ✿ Get scary thoughts stuck in your head

- ✿ Don't want to leave your parents or carer because you are worried

- ✿ Feel tired or ill because of worrying

- ✿ Miss out on fun activities because of worrying

If that sounds like you (maybe a lot of the time, or maybe only sometimes), this book is jam-packed with activities and advice to help you beat your worries, feel braver and become more confident. You can do them at your own pace, there's no rush!

If you get stuck, or want to talk about anything you see in this book, you can ask a trusted adult for help, or just for them to listen. That grown-up could be your mom or dad, your carer, one of your teachers, a big brother or sister, grandparent, aunt, uncle, next-door neighbour, or any other adult that you know well and feel comfortable talking to.

INTRODUCING FIZ THE MONSTER

Hello! I'm Fiz and I'm here to help guide you through this book. I'm looking forward to showing you all the activities and new ideas inside! Are you ready? Let's dive on in!

PART 1: WHAT IS ANXIETY?

In this chapter we'll find out all about anxiety: what it is, what it feels like and why we feel it.

Anxiety is an emotion we feel when we are nervous, afraid and worried all in one go.

ACTIVITY: ALL ABOUT ME!

First let's find out about you and what's important to you.

My name is...

I am __ years old.

My family members are...

My favorite thing is...

For fun I like to...

I'm really good at...

I LOVE MYSELF

What are feelings?

Human beings can have loads of different feelings, and another word for feelings is emotions. Sometimes emotions change because of the things going on around us, and sometimes they change because of our thoughts.

- ✿ Emotions can feel small and quiet or big and loud. Some feelings feel good, and some feel bad

- ✿ Everyone has feelings, and you can't always tell what someone's feeling from looking at them

- ✿ When you are feeling an emotion, it can feel like the emotion is taking over your whole body, which can lead to you having emotions and thoughts that are not very nice

- ✿ It's OK to feel whatever you are feeling, even if it's one of those emotions that doesn't feel very nice, like sadness or anger

We give names to the different ways we feel inside so we can talk about them with others. Think about what color each emotion would be if they were colors and use that color to shade in the bubbles.

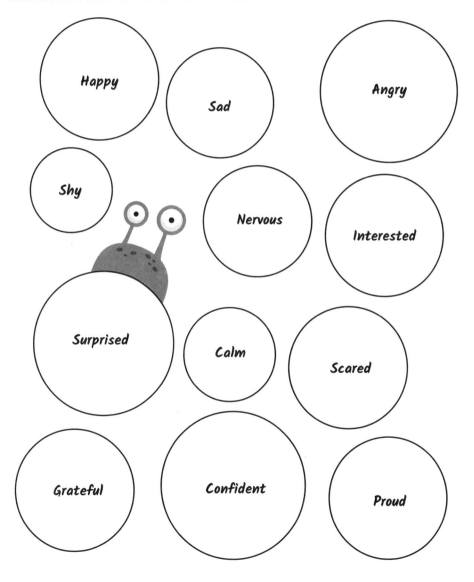

Can you think of any more emotions? Write some other ideas you might have in these bubbles.

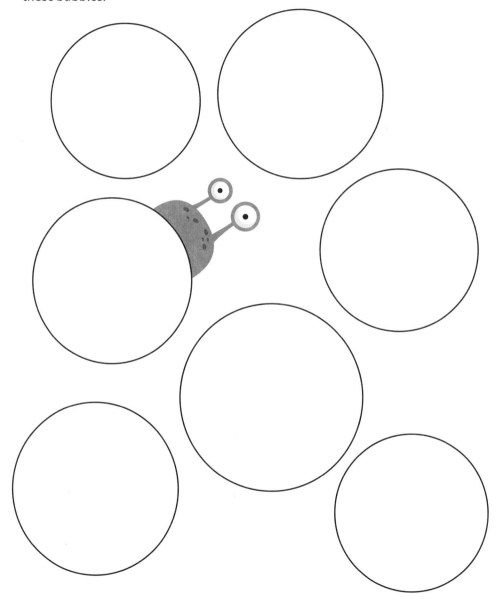

Why do we feel worried?

Everyone feels many different feelings every day, and sometimes the less happy feelings that we've just read about take up more space in our thoughts and this can make us worried. How do you feel right now? (Write as many feelings as you like.)

E.g., calm, sad, hungry…

Anxiety is the feeling you get when you have a worry that you can't get out of your mind, one that starts to be part of your thoughts so that you don't have time to think about other things. You might feel anxious that something that has happened in the past will happen again, or that something bad will happen to you or someone you love. Perhaps you're so scared of the dark that you get a horrible feeling in your body when you think about it.

Sometimes, people get anxious and they can't really explain why, or they don't think anyone else will understand their worries.

Anxiety is just one of the emotions humans feel, and it's normal! In fact, it's a really important emotion that can keep you safe and help you make sensible choices. Humans evolved to feel scared and nervous to keep us safe from danger.

All these emotions could be linked with anxiety

In the Stone Age this meant watching out for saber-toothed tigers…

Today, worrying helps remind us to be careful in the same way.

I CAN TRY SOMETHING NEW

ACTIVITY: HOW DOES FIZ FEEL?

Fiz's friends are running away—they say they don't want to play with Fiz today. Write down how you think Fiz feels.

_____

_____

_____

_____

_____

Great answers! When others are unkind it can make us feel all sorts of emotions. We often remember unhappy moments for a long time after, and might worry about them happening again.

What does anxiety feel like?

We feel anxious when we feel a mixture of worried, nervous and afraid. We can feel anxiety all over our bodies:

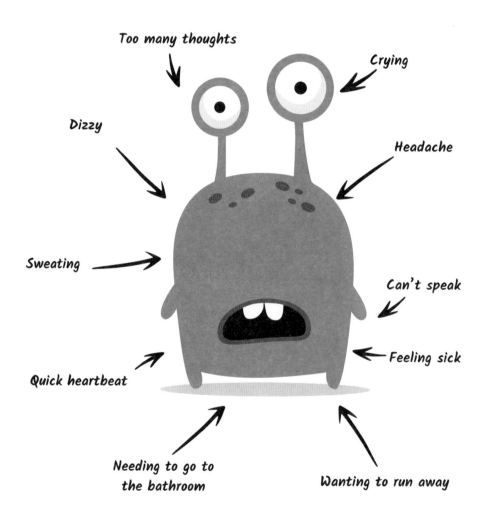

Too many thoughts

Crying

Dizzy

Headache

Sweating

Can't speak

Quick heartbeat

Feeling sick

Needing to go to the bathroom

Wanting to run away

What do kids worry about?

If you have worries, you are not alone. All children worry, and you can't tell from looking at someone what their worries are. Here are some of the things kids your age worry about:

- ✿ Criminals

- ✿ Ghosts

- ✿ Being left at home by yourself

- ✿ Dying

- ✿ Getting ill

- ✿ Doing badly at school

- ✿ Being sick at school

- ✿ Friends leaving you out

Some of these might sound scary to you, and some might seem like no big deal. The things you worry about might not be on that list. Brains are very complicated, and everyone worries about different things!

There are lots of different kinds of anxiety...

🌸 Some children feel very anxious about something in particular

🌸 Some children feel a bit anxious all the time, with lots of small worries that seem to fill up their minds

🌸 Some children feel anxious about being away from their parents, or about meeting new people

🌸 Some children feel anxious that bad things will happen to them or to people they love

🌸 Some children feel they need to check or organize things because they think something bad will happen if they don't

Some children feel anxious because they imagine themselves doing something bad, hurting themselves or someone else. If you have these horrible thoughts, remember: **thoughts aren't facts**. Just because you are imagining these things does not mean they will come true. Take a break and take some deep breaths. If you talk to a trusted grown-up about your worries they can help you to deal with these types of thoughts.

If something bad happened to you or someone you love, it can sometimes make you feel anxious that it was your fault, or that it will happen again. This is a normal reaction and the best way to help you feel less worried is to talk about it. An adult you feel comfortable talking to will be able to listen to you and help you understand your worries better.

EVERYONE FEELS WORRIED SOMETIMES

ACTIVITY: MY WORRIES

Everyone feels worried or anxious about different things. There might be one thing that makes you feel anxious, or there might be many things. Here are just two examples:

Harry feels anxious about being sick. If he hears about another person being sick he gets very nervous about catching germs. When he feels this way he doesn't eat properly and washes his hands more than he needs to.

Natalia feels anxious that there is something under her bed. She feels stuck because when it's dark she is scared to check and scared to get out of bed and tell her parents. She has trouble getting to sleep sometimes because she can't stop thinking about it.

When do you feel anxious? E.g., when I'm away from my mom. Write or draw as many as you like here:

How do you act when you are feeling anxious? Write or draw as many actions as you like here:

E.g., I stay close to my dad and ask him often when Mom will be back, and if she's OK.

Sometimes, when we feel anxious, we act in ways that make us feel better for a little while, but that won't help change how we feel about that situation. Because we feel the same about the situation, our anxious thoughts will come back just the same next time. Later in the book (page 67) we'll look at ways to beat anxiety by helping you change how you act and think when you feel anxious.

Panic attacks

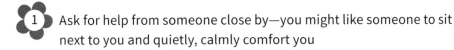

Sometimes anxiety can feel so big that you feel your body is out of control. This is called a **panic attack.**

You might feel dizzy, hot or sick, and your heart might beat faster during a panic attack.

Even though they feel horrible and scary, panic attacks can't hurt you. If you feel like you might be having one, there are things you can do to help you cope while it passes:

1 Ask for help from someone close by—you might like someone to sit next to you and quietly, calmly comfort you

2 Close your eyes

3 Remember that the panic attack will end soon, and that it can't hurt you

4 Think about your breathing. Count to five as you take a deep breath, then let it out slowly: 1, 2, 3, 4, 5

5 Once the panic attack has passed, you might feel tired or thirsty. Don't rush, take a moment to relax until you are ready to go back to what you were doing

Later in the book (page 41) we'll look at lots of special ways to calm down when your anxiety gets too much.

BAD FEELINGS ARE NORMAL AND THEY SOON PASS

PART 2: DEALING WITH WORRIES

In this chapter we'll find out more about how anxiety feels, and discover some tricks to help you feel calmer.

What is anxiety?

ACTIVITY: HAPPY BRAIN/WORRIED BRAIN

How does your brain feel when you're happy? What kind of things do you think about?

E.g., my family, a fun memory, my favorite hobby. Write, draw and color in your happy brain here:

How does your brain feel when you're anxious? What kinds of things do you think about?

E.g., an unhappy memory, something I'm scared will happen. Write, draw and color in your anxious brain here:

Your happy brain and your worried brain look quite different from each other, don't they? Different thoughts can make us feel different emotions, and our brains behave differently depending on what emotion we're feeling.

I AM ALLOWED TO MAKE MISTAKES

Listen to your body and mind

When you feel anxious, the feeling comes from the part of your brain which controls your emotions. If your brain senses danger (even if it's not really dangerous, just something that you feel worried about) the control centre sends signals all around your body, which cause things like a fast heartbeat, sweating and feeling sick.

When you feel that anxious feeling starting to build in your body, don't panic! Here are some quick tricks you can do anywhere to help yourself feel calmer.

* ❀ Count backwards from ten

* ❀ Think about the ground right under your shoes, can you feel it? What does it feel like?

* ❀ Imagine you have a mug of hot chocolate in front of you. Breathe in to smell it, blow out to cool it down

* ❀ Shut your eyes and imagine a beautiful garden—what kinds of flowers and plants are in the garden? Try to notice lots of little details

* ❀ Take a moment to notice four things around you that you can see, then three you can hear, two you can touch and one you can smell—say the name of each thing you've noticed either out loud or to yourself

IF YOU HAVE WORRIES AND YOU DON'T KNOW WHAT TO DO, ASK FOR HELP

The anxiety hill

When anxiety starts to build inside you, it can feel really scary. Anxiety usually goes in the shape of a hill, like this:

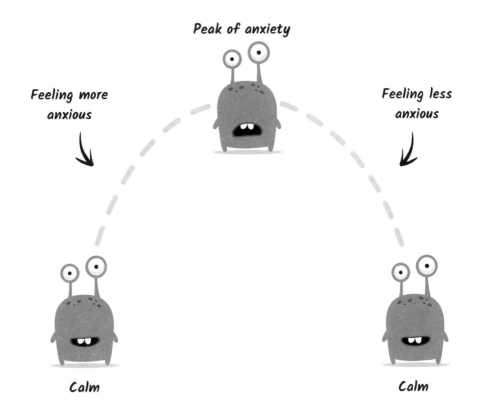

If you feel your anxiety start going up the hill, imagine this picture: the top of the hill is the point when you feel most anxious. Once you reach this point it's important to know that your anxiety will not last for a long time and it will go back down the other side, so you will feel calmer and calmer until the anxiety has gone.

ACTIVITY: HANDPRINT BREATHING

You can do this very simple exercise anywhere, any time. The small act of stopping to breathe can calm you down and help you feel less anxious.

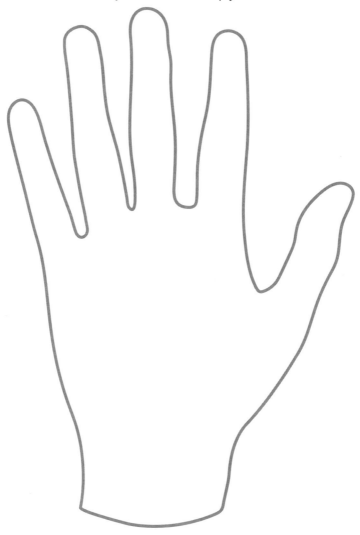

✿ Stretch your hand out on the outline of the hand on the previous page

✿ With the pointing finger of your other hand, trace up and down your fingers

✿ Breathe in as you trace up

✿ Hold your breath at the tip of your finger

✿ And breathe out as you trace down

✿ Keep going until you have traced all five of your fingers

You can even make your own handprint breathing picture! Put your hand on a piece of paper and draw around it, or cover your hand in paint and press firmly down to make a handprint. You can decorate your hand shape any way you like, cut it out and keep it with you to use whenever you need to.

ACTIVITY: MY BATTLE CRY!

Anxiety is a tough thing to beat, and you don't have to do it by yourself! You're a team with your family and all the other people you love and trust.

Why not come up with a battle cry to help you feel determined and brave enough to beat anxiety?

Fiz's battle cry is… I CAN DO THIS!

Your battle cry can be whatever works for you. It could be the same as Fiz's, you could make up your own, or maybe pick one of these ideas:

Can you think of any other battle cries? Write them down here:

Practice saying your battle cry ten times at different volumes with someone you trust joining in. It might feel strange at first, but it will also help you feel confident and ready for anything.

ACTIVITY: COUNT IT OUT

If you're feeling anxious, it can be hard to get your mind off those anxious thoughts. It's helpful to have a special game you can play any time to take your mind off those anxious thoughts and feelings.

When anxiety strikes, Fiz likes to count things that are around:

You can count anything, including:

- ✿ Electrical sockets

- ✿ Birds

- ✿ Chairs

- ✿ People

- ✿ Pictures on the wall

- ✿ Trees

- ✿ Cars

- ✿ Shopping bags

Counting like this means you have to concentrate, which keeps your brain busy. A busy brain has less time for anxious thoughts, so they can more easily escape from your mind.

How big is my problem?

When something happens that makes you feel anxious, the problem can feel absolutely ginormous! It feels like it's taking up your whole brain sometimes. Stop! Take a moment to work out the real size of your problem. If it's a really big problem, you'll probably need to find someone to help. But usually, problems aren't as big as they first feel.

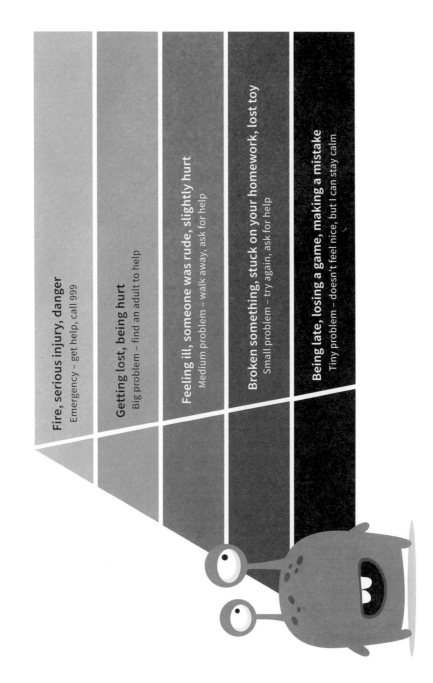

Fire, serious injury, danger
Emergency – get help, call 999

Getting lost, being hurt
Big problem – find an adult to help

Feeling ill, someone was rude, slightly hurt
Medium problem – walk away, ask for help

Broken something, stuck on your homework, lost toy
Small problem – try again, ask for help

Being late, losing a game, making a mistake
Tiny problem – doesn't feel nice, but I can stay calm

ACTIVITY: MY DAY

What do you do in the morning? Eat breakfast, brush your teeth, get your school things ready… do you do it in the same order every day? Having a routine can help you feel calm and in control. If you know what's coming next and have a plan for each day, it can help you worry less. If you don't have a routine right now, you could create one with your parents.

Can you draw your morning, after-school or evening routine as a comic strip?

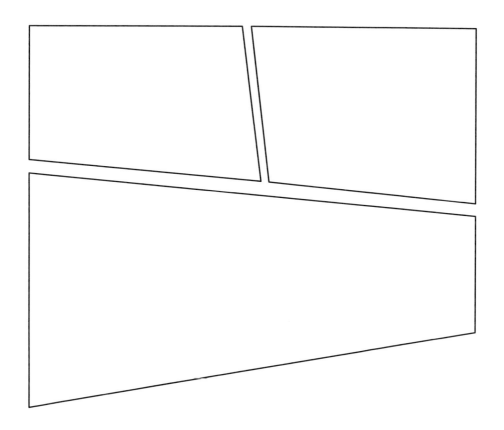

I WILL BE PATIENT WITH MYSELF

The big wide world

Sometimes we hear about bad things which are happening in the world, and it can feel like the world is a big and frightening place. You might feel anxious about some of the things you learn about at school or in the news. It's important to remember that the news is made of mostly the bad things that happen in the world.

At any time, most of the seven billion people in the world are having normal days, a lot of people are having really good days, and a few are having very bad days—we usually only hear about those few people having really bad days.

If the news was about all the good things that are happening in the world every single day, there wouldn't be time to get through them all!

If you work with others to show kindness, bravery and generosity, **you can change the world**. If you see unfairness happening in your town, at school or somewhere else in the world there is always something you can do to help.

It feels good to help others, and it will help you feel less anxious and more confident when you realise what you can achieve. Even if it feels like something small, small good things add up, and inspire others to show kindness and bravery too!

Things that go bump in the night

Do you enjoy scary books or TV shows? Some people love to be scared by these! But sometimes a scary story or character can stick in your mind and make you feel anxious about things you know don't exist. It's always OK to take a break from something that scares you, even if you know it's something made-up like ghosts, monsters or zombies.

You might even feel that you ought to like scary things because your friends do, when in truth you don't enjoy being scared. Remember there are lots of people like you who just decide that scary isn't for them.

Even monsters get scared by other monsters

Knowledge is power

If there's something spooky and supernatural that makes you feel anxious, like ghosts or vampires, you might find it helps to become an expert!

When you're feeling calm and brave, find out all you can about the subject. Try to look at books or websites that aren't scary to you—can you find any funny or cute examples? Ask lots of questions, and if you can't find an answer, you can create your own, like:

What do ghosts eat for breakfast?

What makes a werewolf cry?

Do vampires lose their baby teeth like we do, and does the tooth fairy visit them?

Can you think of some expert questions and answers? Write them down here:

_____

_____

_____

_____

_____

_____

_____

_____

_____

Why do we tell scary stories?

Throughout history, people have invented stories about monsters and ghosts to put a face on something they are frightened of, but can't explain or control.

If you're feeling anxious about something supernatural, it might be a good time to sit down and confide in a grown-up about the things that are worrying you in your life. Often by doing this, you will feel calmer and more able to control anxiety about things outside of the real world.

ANXIETY COMES FROM A HEALTHY BRAIN WITH A BIG IMAGINATION

Keep a diary

Lots of people keep a diary for all kinds of reasons. A diary can be really useful if you experience anxiety—all you need is a notebook and a pencil. It can be secret or, if you want to, you can show a trusted grown-up.

With a diary, you can:

✿ Take annoying thoughts out of your head and put them into the diary

✿ Break big worries down into a list of small tasks

✿ Keep track of your anxiety—write down what happened each time you felt anxious

✿ Write about all the good things that happen too!

It can be useful to go back through your diary to see if you can spot a pattern for when you feel anxious. You could do this by yourself, but it might help to share the job with an adult you feel comfortable with.

ACTIVITY: HELP FIZ FEEL BETTER

Fiz feels anxious when there's a dog nearby. If Fiz is playing at the park and a dog arrives, Fiz wants to leave, even if it's a small and well-behaved dog.

What would you say to help Fiz feel better about dogs?

_____

_____

_____

_____

_____

_____

Thoughts, feelings and actions

How we think, how we feel and how we act are all linked. For example, Fiz thinks all dogs will bark and jump up, so Fiz feels afraid, and leaves the park.

Thought	Feeling	Action
All dogs will bark and jump	*Afraid*	*Leaves the park*

Everyone has different thoughts, feelings and actions. Here are some other ways people might think, feel and act when they see a dog at the park:

Thought	Feeling	Action
What a sweet dog *Dogs are OK*	*Excited* *Uninterested*	*Asks to stroke the dog* *Carries on with game*

Can you remember a time you felt anxious? What did you **think**? What did you **feel**? What did you **do**?

Thought	Feeling	Action
↓	↓	↓

_____   _____   _____

What's going wrong to make Fiz feel so anxious? Fiz is having something called a **thinking error**.

Thinking errors are when your brain gets mixed up, and there are lots of different types which we'll look at on the next page.

The more times you have one of these mix-ups, the more you believe the thought is true.

Fiz is having a thinking error called *Fortune Telling*—thinking you can see the future, and thinking something bad will definitely happen!

It's tricky when you're feeling anxious, but when you think calmly and carefully, you realise that it's not true. Just because a dog barked at Fiz once, doesn't mean it will happen again.

Thinking errors

Let's look at the most common types of thinking error:

Focus on the negatives: I can only see the bad parts—even when something nice happens, I always find a way to feel bad about it

All-or-nothing thinking: If something isn't perfect, I've failed completely

Magnified thinking: If a small, bad thing happens, it feels really big and important

Mind reading: I know everyone thinks badly of me

Fortune-telling: I know something will go wrong, so I won't try

Feelings are facts: I feel bad, so I must *be* bad at everything I do

Putting yourself down: I'm terrible!

Unrealistic expectations: I should be perfect at everything

Blaming yourself: It's all my fault!

Do any of these thought mix-ups sound like the voice you talk to yourself with? Draw a circle around any that you recognize.

Remember, these kinds of thoughts are **thinking errors** and they are not true, just your brain getting mixed up. When you can recognize these mix-ups you can start to question them. The best idea is to talk them over with a trusted adult—quite often, talking about them can help you understand the mix-up better. In the next chapter (page 67) we'll learn how to stop these mix-ups and think more calmly and clearly.

I CAN ASK
FOR HELP

PART 3: SOLVING THE PROBLEM

Get ready to find out how to tackle anxiety and change the way you think, feel and act to become a calmer, happier you!

Fact or opinion?

You're doing so brilliantly well! Now it's time to find out all about how anxiety works.

Do you know the difference between a fact and an opinion? Facts are things that are always true, no matter what anyone says, thinks or wishes. Opinions are things we think or feel—someone else might think or feel differently. Here are some examples:

Fact: The sun is hot
Opinion: Summer is the best season

Fact: Humans need water to live
Opinion: Water is a boring drink

Fact: Cats can't talk
Opinion: Cats are better than dogs

ACTIVITY: FACTS ABOUT ME

Can you write some facts about you?
E.g., my hair color is…

Can you write some of your opinions?
E.g., the best subject at school is…

I WILL DO
MY BEST

Thoughts aren't facts

Just because you think something, doesn't make it true. If you feel anxious about something, it can feel very real and very true, but remember: **You are stronger than your worry.**

You can **think** that the sky is green or bananas are purple or there's a monster under your bed, but if you look around at the world, you will find that these thoughts aren't **facts.** You can **think** that you're going to do badly in your spelling test, or come last in a race on sports day, but thinking that doesn't mean it's going to happen.

Fact: Mike can skip

Opinion: Mike is the best at skipping

We've talked about how thoughts aren't facts, and how thinking something bad will happen doesn't mean it will actually happen. But what if it did happen? What if a dog barks, or you do badly in a test, or your mum's late to pick you up from school? Would you be OK? You would be fine. It might not be very nice, but you will be OK. What's more, you can make a plan for what you would do if your worry comes true. Here's an example for you:

Kate worries every week that her mum will forget to pick her up from gymnastics club. Kate's mum has never been late to pick her up, but Kate can't get the worry out of her head. She's thinking of giving up gymnastics because she feels so anxious about it. Kate tells her mum how she feels, and Kate's mum listens. They make a plan, just in case Kate's mum is ever late:

🌼 *Kate will stay with her teacher*

🌼 *The teacher will phone Kate's mum*

🌼 *The teacher will stay with Kate until her mum arrives*

If you have a worry like Kate, you could try making your own plan. Sit down with an adult you can confide in and talk about your worry, and make a plan just in case it happens. This will help you understand that you will be OK, even if your worry comes true.

✿ _____

✿ _____

✿ _____

✿ _____

✿ _____

✿ _____

✿ _____

✿ _____

✿ _____

✿ _____

✿ _____

Work it out!

Sometimes, when we get anxious, we can't tell straight away why we are feeling that way. Take a moment to listen to your body and your thoughts.

- ❀ Where can you feel the anxiety?

- ❀ What are you worried will happen?

- ❀ Where has that idea come from?

Once you know what is making you feel anxious, think about breaking it down into smaller pieces. Here's an example:

Amir is feeling anxious in his head and in his tummy. He's imagining his teacher being angry with him on Monday. Amir feels anxious because he has three pieces of homework to do this weekend, but hasn't started yet.

First, Amir needs to take a deep breath. Then he thinks how he can break down his problem into smaller steps. Here's his plan:

Straight away: He can make a list to plan when he will do each piece of homework

Later today: He can do one piece of homework at a time

Next time: He can plan some time each weekend to spend on homework

Why don't you have a go at writing or drawing some thoughts in the same way as Amir?

- **Straight away:**
  _____
  _____
  _____

- **Later today:**
  _____
  _____
  _____

- **Next time:**
  _____
  _____
  _____

CHALLENGES ARE FUN

ACTIVITY: WHAT DOES YOUR WORRY LOOK LIKE?

What does your anxious feeling look like? Can you draw or write about it below? It could be a type of weather, monster, animal, person, shape or robot—use your imagination, you can even give it a name!

Talk to your worry

Now you've drawn your worry, can you imagine yourself talking to it?

If you are feeling anxious, the first thing to do is to take a deep breath and let a calm feeling into your mind. You could use the handprint breathing exercise on page 44 to help you.

Once you feel calm enough, you can ask your worry questions to find the facts:

Once you have taken the time to ask yourself these questions, you'll see that you feel less anxious. Watch how Fiz talks to a worry on the next page to see how it's done.

Understanding your worries

Fiz thought that the dog would bark and jump up. Now let's talk to that worry and look for some facts:

Is that a fact or an opinion?
I'm not sure.

Is the dog barking now?
No.

What am I thinking?
The dog will bark and jump up at me.

Am I having a thought mix-up?
Yes – I am thinking that all dogs will bark and jump up, but it's not true!

What is the worst thing that could happen?
The dog barks and jumps up at me.

If that happens, will I be OK?
Yes – it will feel scary but the dog's owner will make sure I'm not hurt.

What is the best thing that could happen?
The dog is well behaved and I carry on having fun at the park.

What will probably happen?
The dog might bark a bit, but that's just a noise. It won't jump up at me because I will stay in the playground.

I CAN
BOUNCE BACK

Mindfulness

✿ Mindfulness is a way of thinking about the world that was invented by people called Buddhists. It means paying attention to what is happening and how we feel at this exact moment. Being mindful can help us feel calmer and is a great way to deal with big feelings.

✿ When we think mindfully, we see our thoughts and emotions as they pass through our minds and bodies like clouds passing through the sky. Everything you think or feel is OK, and it can't hurt you.

Try this mindfulness exercise, you can practice it any time:

Find somewhere quiet and comfortable to sit.

Count ten breaths, then open your eyes.

Close your eyes and imagine your thoughts are clouds floating across the sky.

Stay in your tummy and concentrate on how breathing makes it go up and down.

Notice the clouds' shapes and colors.

Now, take your attention down into your tummy. Thoughts live in your head, there are no thoughts in your tummy.

See what happens when you try this… you will most likely feel calm and less worried.

ACTIVITY: MY WORRY JAR

Worrying is really annoying! Sometimes you just want to put your worries away for a while and have a break. Write a worry in one of the spaces:

Now carefully cut it out (or ask an adult to help), fold it in half and keep it in a jar. Once the lid is on, the worries are stuck inside and can't bother you. There are two spaces on the previous page, but remember you can write a worry down on scrap paper and pop it in your jar any time.

I AM NOT A GLASS BAUBLE. I AM A BOUNCY BALL!

ACTIVITY: I'M BRAVE!

Now it's time to be really brave. Being brave isn't about never feeling afraid—true bravery means feeling scared, but facing our fears and doing it anyway. In the next few pages we're going to see how being brave can help you conquer anxiety.

Can you think of a time you were really brave? Write or draw about it here:

Letting go

Now we're going to look at how to let go of anxious behaviors. Sometimes we do things too much because we are anxious about what will happen if we don't. Let's see how Fatima can change her anxious behavior into brave behavior...

Fatima's favorite toy is a teddy bear. She has just started at a new school and has been bringing the toy to school with her in secret. One day, a teacher finds the toy and tells Fatima it's against the rules to bring toys from home. Fatima feels panicked and sick when she thinks about going to school without her little bear. She thinks something bad will happen to her if she doesn't have the toy with her. What should Fatima do?

Leaving the toy at home straight away feels too upsetting to Fatima, but the thought of getting in trouble at school makes her feel even worse. Fatima decides to talk to her parents about her problem, and they come up with a plan.

First, Fatima asks her worry some questions to find the facts.

Fatima's bravery plan

Next, Fatima and her parents make a plan to help build up Fatima's bravery over a few weeks.

1. Bring the toy to school but only have it out at break times

2. Bring the toy to school, then give it to Mom when it's time to go into my classroom

3. Hold the toy until we get to my school's street

4. Hold the toy until the end of my street

5. Let Mom hold the toy – I can hold it two times for one minute each

6. Let Mom hold the toy – I can hold it once

7. Let Mom hold the toy – I can ask for it if I need it

8. Let Mom hold the toy – try not to ask for it

9. Leave the toy at home

Fatima plans to take small steps towards her goal, each time getting a little bit braver. If it takes a few days for Fatima to be ready to take the next step, that's OK! By the end of the steps she'll feel brave enough to leave the toy at home.

Face your fears

Sometimes we avoid doing fun or interesting things because we are anxious about what will happen. Let's see how Joe finds the bravery to try something he's nervous about…

When Joe thinks about swimming, it makes him feel nervous and he starts to sweat. He worries that he will sink to the bottom of the swimming pool, and that water will get in his eyes. Next term, Joe's class will be having swimming lessons at the local pool. Joe wants to be able to swim, but he also feels very anxious about going in the water. What should Joe do?

Joe talks to his parents about his problem, and they come up with a plan together.

First, Joe asks his worry some questions to find the facts.

Joe feels a bit better, but he still feels anxious about swimming, because he knows that water can be dangerous, and the absolute worst thing that could happen is that he could drown.

So the first thing Joe does is to find out how likely *that is, and he discovers that it's very unlikely to happen. On top of this, he finds out that the best way to avoid the dangers of water is to learn how to swim safely with a qualified swimming teacher.*

Joe's bravery plan

Next, Joe and his parents come up with small steps to reach Joe's goal.

1. Research how to stay safe when swimming

2. Visit the swimming pool, but don't go in the water

3. Choose myself new goggles from the shop

4. Go to the pool, get changed and sit on the edge

5. Dip my feet into the water

6. Get into the water at the shallow end with one of my parents, with my goggles on, where I can touch the bottom

7. Try using a swimming float in the shallow end with one of my parents

8. Splash water on my face

9. Put my head under the water for one second

Joe plans to face his fear a little bit at a time. He doesn't rush and some steps might take longer to get used to than others. At the end of his bravery plan he'll feel ready to join in with his class's swimming lessons!

ACTIVITY: MY BRAVERY PLAN

Think about what makes you feel anxious. Can you design your own bravery plan to deal with your anxiety?

1. _____
   _____

2. _____
   _____

3. _____
   _____

4. _____
   _____

5. _____
   _____

6. _____
   _____

I AM
NOT THE
ONLY ONE

PART 4: LOOKING AFTER YOURSELF

You've been working really hard, and should be really proud of yourself! We are strongest when we take good care of our bodies, so it's super important to take time to relax and make sure your body's getting everything it needs.

What do you do to relax?

Taking time to relax is really important for keeping healthy and happy. Why not try one of these chilled-out activities:

- ✿ Paint a pebble with acrylic paint

- ✿ Make a collage

- ✿ Do some gentle stretches

- ✿ Read a book

- ✿ Write a poem

- ✿ Go for a bike ride

- ✿ Watch a candle-flame flickering (ask an adult for help with this!)

- ✿ Listen to some music

- ✿ Watch the clouds—what shapes can you spot?

- ✿ Collect some flowers and leaves from your garden, then draw them

Can you think of some more? Draw or write some of your own ideas here:

Unplug yourself

✿ Watching TV or playing online games can be fun, but all that excitement can be stressful for your brain. Try to spend time doing fun real-world activities like building or making things with friends, drawing, reading or playing outside with your family.

What is tension?

Scrunch up your face, so your nose is wrinkled and lines appear between your eyebrows. Now relax and let your face go back to normal.

Did you feel your whole body change when you relaxed your face muscles? When your face was scrunched up, that was tension. When you let it go back to normal, that's relaxation.

When we feel anxious or upset we often feel tension in our bodies. You can learn tricks to help you let tension out of your body.

ACTIVITY: SQUEEZY NOSE BREATHING

Taking a deep breath is a great way to make yourself feel better any time. Squeezy nose breathing helps you take deep, slow breaths, and will make you feel calm.

- ✿ First, squish down your right nostril

- ✿ Take a deep breath in through your left nostril

- ✿ Now hold the breath, and swap hands so you're squishing down your left nostril

- ✿ Breathe out through your right nostril

- ✿ Now do it again, the other way round

- ✿ Keep going for five breaths from each nostril

I CAN
TRY AGAIN

Appearances

Some people think that the way you look is important. Every day we see people on TV and in magazines looking flawless. But did you know, that's not how those people look in real life? Special lights on TV and computer effects on photographs mean that normal human beings can look like aliens from Planet Perfect!

Spending ages trying to look perfect is a waste of time. There are a million more interesting things to do and think about, plus **you don't exist for people to look at**! You're already the best and only version of you anyway.

ACTIVITY: MIRROR, MIRROR

Next time you look in the mirror, notice something you like about yourself, and say something nice!

Here's some inspiration:

Can you think of some more? Write them down in the mirrors below:

Love your body

Your body is incredible. Did you know…?

- ✿ Once you've lost your baby teeth, your new teeth are just as strong as a shark's teeth

- ✿ Your heart beats over 100,000 times every day

- ✿ As well as having unique finger prints, humans also have unique tongue prints

- ✿ All 37 trillion of the cells in your body work together to keep you breathing, laughing and learning

Your body naturally changes as you get older and start to grow into an adult, which might make you feel worried or embarrassed. Remember these changes are normal, and they happen to everyone.

It's common to feel shy about your body, and remember that no-one but you is allowed to see or touch your body without your permission. You can always talk to your parents or a trusted teacher about anything that's troubling or confusing you.

Keep healthy

Eating healthily and drinking plenty of water are two of the most important things you can do to keep yourself growing, learning and happy! When you look after your body, you will naturally feel calmer and have more energy.

We are made of over 60 per cent water, and it's always coming out of our bodies one way or another—when we sweat, breathe out, cry or go to the toilet. You need to drink at least six to eight glasses of water to keep your body in tip-top shape and well hydrated. To stay healthy you should also eat five pieces of fruit or vegetables every day.

ACTIVITY: SLEEP

Getting plenty of sleep will help you feel calmer, happier and give you more energy during the day. Sleep gives your brain time to work out everything that has happened to you or been on your mind during the daytime. Often problems which are bugging you during the day can seem a lot more manageable after a good night's sleep!

What would your dream bedroom look like? Can you draw or write about it here?

> ✿ **Try to get plenty of sleep every night.**

Do you ever have trouble getting to sleep? Try this trick:

1 Lie on your back with your toes pointed

2 Now slowly lift your feet until your toes are pointing at the ceiling

3 Let your feet sink back down very, very slowly

4 Do this five times and you'll feel relaxed and sleepy

PART 5: FRIENDSHIPS AND BULLYING

Friends are brilliant and super-important, but sometimes friendships can be hard work and make us feel anxious.

What makes a true friend?

True friends are the best—they're the people that make us smile, the ones we love to spend time with most in the world.

But sometimes, someone might say they're your friend but not act like a friend at all.

Just because someone spends time with you and says they are your friend, doesn't make it true! False friends are like bullies in disguise. Remember: you don't have to spend time with people who are unkind to you.

A true friend:

✿ Listens to you

✿ Talks to you kindly

✿ Stands up for you

✿ Includes you

A false friend:

✿ Ignores you

✿ Leaves you out

✿ Hurts you

✿ Teases or embarrasses you

I DESERVE
GOOD FRIENDS

What does bullying look like?

Bullying can happen in lots of different ways, and it can happen in real life or on the internet.

Bullying can be:

✿ Hurting, embarrassing or upsetting you on purpose

✿ Taking your belongings without permission

✿ Making you do something you don't want to do

✿ Gossiping or telling lies about you

✿ Calling you names or teasing you

✿ Pushing and shoving

✿ Leaving you out

✿ It can also be any other behaviors that make you feel unhappy or anxious

If you are being bullied, it's not your fault. Talk to a trusted adult about what is happening. You are important and you deserve to be treated with respect.

You're not alone

Sometimes, you might think you're the only one who feels the way you do. But remember, you can't see inside other people's heads. Each person you meet has their own worries and their own favorite things, and you can't always tell how someone is feeling from looking at them.

Even if you feel really alone with your worries, you are not, and there are always people around you who can help.

TODAY IS GOING TO BE A REALLY GOOD DAY

We are all different!

Everyone's different, and that's what makes life interesting! From our favorite book to what scares us, no two people are the same.

What differences can you see on the outside? Freckles, skin color, glasses, short or long hair… these things don't tell us anything about what that person is like on the inside. Just because Fiz has freckles, doesn't mean Fiz likes the same things or has the same thoughts as other freckly monsters.

What differences are invisible? How friendly someone is, what their favorite breakfast cereal is, what they worry about… you only find these things out when you get to know someone's **personality**.

ACTIVITY: LOVE YOUR DIFFERENCES!

Think of one of your good friends, what do you have in common with them? How are they different to you?

We have these things in common...	We are different in these ways...
Example: *My favorite food is pasta and my friend's favorite food is pasta too*	Example: *My favorite subject at school is English but my friend's favorite subject is science*

We have these things in common…	We are different in these ways…

Even though you are different in some ways, you still love to spend time together. It's OK to be yourself—it's the only person you can truly be!

EVERYONE HAS THEIR OWN SPECIAL WAY OF BEING THEMSELVES

My perfect friend...?

It might seem like one of your friends has a perfect life. If only your hair, house, computer or shoes were more like theirs, your life would be so much better, right? Wrong! Happiness comes from inside. Getting something new can feel good for a little while, but soon that feeling disappears and you go back to feeling like you did before you got it.

We only see what other people choose to show about themselves. No one is perfect, because perfect doesn't exist.

We are all lucky in different ways. It can be hard to remember the ways in which you are lucky, especially when you're feeling low.

ACTIVITY: I'M GRATEFUL FOR...

Being grateful is feeling and showing you're thankful when you are lucky or other people do something kind for you. Fill out the spaces below with things you are grateful for and the challenges that you are facing.

Can you list 10 things you're grateful for this week? They can be big or small:
E.g., a yummy breakfast, a warm home

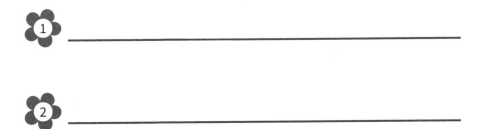

1 _____

2 _____

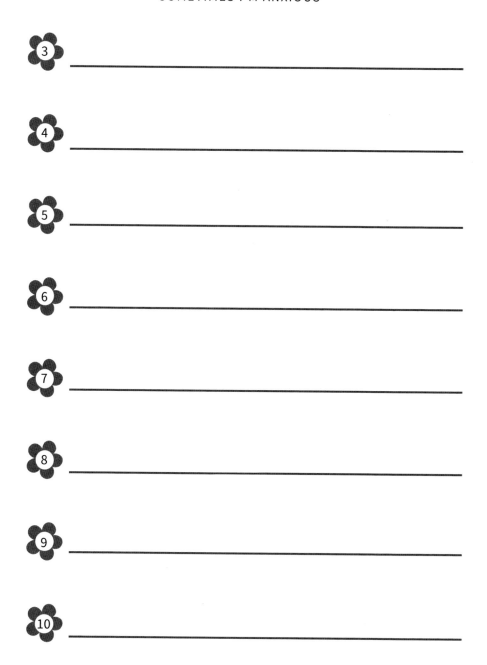

3 _____

4 _____

5 _____

6 _____

7 _____

8 _____

9 _____

10 _____

What are you finding tricky right now?

E.g., a disagreement with a friend

What are you learning from these challenges?

E.g., how to find a solution everyone is happy with

People I'm grateful for:

1. _____

2. _____

3. _____

4. _____

5. _____

The best part of today was...

This is a great activity to do at the end of the day. You could even get in the habit of writing a few things you're grateful for every time you write in your diary (page 60).

LIFE'S AN ADVENTURE, NOT A COMPETITION

PART 6: WHAT NEXT?

Wow! You've learned so much and hopefully found some great tricks to help you beat anxiety. You've learned all about how your thoughts, feelings and actions work together, and how to relax. Now it's time to put your new skills into practice.

It's normal to feel anxious sometimes—everyone does! Your anxiety won't disappear overnight, and it might be hard work finding new thinking habits and trying things that make you feel nervous.

Remember, you don't have to do this on your own—if you need help you can look again at this book, talk to a trusted grown-up or simply take a break to relax.

ACTIVITY: MY ANXIETY ACTION PLAN

Here's a space to recap and put some of the things you've learned about yourself and your worries all together in an action plan:

My thought mix-ups

Questions for my worry...

My top relaxation tricks

Don't forget to put your bravery plan from page 98 into action!

You're not the only one

Lots of children feel anxious about lots of different things—here are just a few from kids your age.

Isla, 7:

I saw an episode of my favorite TV show with a monster that lives under children's beds. I'm quite brave and I usually like being scared but that one was too scary and I couldn't get to sleep that night. I was really tired the next morning! The next night I felt scared again. I told Mom about it and she put a lamp on the floor, so it was shining under the bed. That made me feel better and I went to sleep after that.

Tilly, 11:

We went on a school trip last month, which was four nights away from our parents. I kept thinking something bad would happen and my parents would get ill or hurt while I was away. Mom and Dad told me not to worry but that didn't stop me worrying! But once I got there I had so much fun with my friends I forgot all about my worries—I'm really glad I did it.

Hassan, 9:

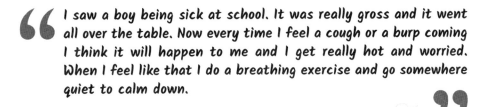

I saw a boy being sick at school. It was really gross and it went all over the table. Now every time I feel a cough or a burp coming I think it will happen to me and I get really hot and worried. When I feel like that I do a breathing exercise and go somewhere quiet to calm down.

Miriam, 8:

Every day I worried about finding someone to sit next to at lunch time. I used to make sure I asked a friend to be a two with me as soon as I got to school in the morning. One day I forgot to ask and had to sit next to someone I didn't know. We chatted and now she's my friend—my worry came true, but I was OK.

Ollie, 8:

I was really worried about catching a horrible disease and dying. I used to spend a long time checking my body to make sure, and asking my parents about different illnesses. I started worrying when my uncle died last year. My parents spoke to me about my uncle, and answered all my questions—now I understand what happened, I don't feel so anxious anymore.

Naomi, 10:

I used to worry about the way I look because I have a birthmark. Now I have a special saying: 'those that matter don't mind, and those that mind don't matter.' It helps me remember that I am special and beautiful just the way I am.

Rowan, 11:

I used to feel anxious all the time about lots of little things. My anxiety was making me feel upset most of the time, so my parents took me to see a friendly doctor who helped us work out how to make me feel better.

Omar, 7:

I don't like PE because I think I will hurt myself. I used to sit on the bench and not join in. Then my friend said he would stay with me and make sure I was OK, so I gave it a try and it's actually quite a lot of fun.

The end

That's it! Fiz is amazed at all the learning you've done together—did you enjoy it too? Remember you can look at this book again any time you like, to remind yourself how anxiety works, or when you need a calming exercise to try.

Give yourself a gigantic pat on the back for all the hard work you've done—you are brave, brilliant and capable of anything you put your mind to!

For parents: How to help your child deal with anxiety

Unfortunately, dealing with anxiety isn't as simple as the title of this book! But there are ways to make life easier for an anxious child. The most important thing you can do is listen to them.

Listen and ask them general questions about school, about their friends and hobbies in an open way, and they'll feel able to talk to you about their fears and worries. Healthy strong relationships with parents and carers help create resilient kids, even if there are a few hiccups along the way. Let them know that you are there for them, that you'll take them seriously and help them solve any problem they come up against—no matter how big or small. When they talk to you about their worries, it's important not to belittle them, but also not to amplify those worries.

Focus on solutions when there's a problem to be solved, and involve your child in finding those solutions. However, sometimes your child might just want to talk about their feelings, so take your cues from them.

If your child becomes panicked or anxious, remember this is their brain telling them that they might be in danger—they aren't being difficult or manipulative. To help them deal with an anxiety attack, you can:

- Come down to their level and take some deep breaths together

- Tell them you understand they're feeling anxious about X

- Hold their hand if they want you to

- Try a counting exercise like Count it out (page 49), or use yours or their hand to do Handprint breathing (page 44)

- Wait until your child is feeling calm, then discuss solutions such as asking their worry questions to find facts

Once they are feeling back to normal, you can talk about what helped during the panic attack, and what didn't, so you are even more prepared next time.

If there's a stressful event coming up—such as a house move—and your child is feeling anxious about it, talk openly with them about what will happen. Look for books or films that will help them understand their feelings—*The Story Cure* by Ella Berthoud and Susan Elderkin is a great resource for finding the right story for every situation. Try to have a daily routine and stick to it: kids feel most secure when they know what comes next.

If your family is going through an upsetting time like a bereavement or divorce, avoid giving your child information they don't need. Try to talk to them using language they'll understand, and encourage them to talk about their feelings and to ask questions—but don't be afraid to admit you don't know all the answers. It can sometimes be easier for children to talk about upsetting subjects when they are occupied with something else, like drawing or coloring. They might even feel more comfortable writing you a letter.

It's natural for loving parents to want to shield their children from negative feelings, but avoiding things that make your child anxious only gives a short-term benefit, while in fact making the problem worse in the long run. The more a situation is avoided, the stronger the child's negative memories and associations with that situation become.

Instead of avoiding, gradually and gently give your child opportunities to form positive memories to associate with the situation. For example, if your child is afraid of the dark, take them camping and toast marshmallows around the campfire after sunset. If they're nervous around water, take them rock pooling. Anxious about public speaking? Put on a play at home.

There are tons of fun ways to gently guide your child towards feeling braver.

If your child asks for reassurance often, try to get to the heart of why they're asking. Talk about the worst-case scenario (and whether they'll be OK if it happens), the best-case scenario, and what is most likely to happen.

Encourage them to try new things, and let them know that it's alright to have a go and not get something right first time.

Finally, let go of guilt—it's tempting to blame ourselves for our children's struggles, or to try to make life as easy as we can for them. Give yourself a break. You're doing a great job by giving your child the tools to grow into a resilient adult.

Further advice

Occasional, short-term anxiety doesn't feel nice, but it is normal. If anxiety starts to interfere with your child's daily life then talk it through with your pediatrician or family doctor. Talk to your child's school if they are struggling with anything school-related. There is no one-size-fits-all solution to anxiety, and it comes in many forms and degrees of severity.

Recommended reading

Starving the Anxiety Gremlin: A Cognitive Behavioral Therapy Workbook for Anxiety Management
Kate Collins-Donnelly
Jessica Kingsley Publishers, 2013

The Story Cure: An A–Z of Books to Keep Kids Happy, Healthy and Wise
Ella Berthoud and Susan Elderkin
Canongate, 2016

Sitting Still Like a Frog: Mindfulness Exercises for Kids (and Their Parents)
Eline Snel
Shambhala, 2013

....

Credits

pp.3, 13, 14, 19, 20, 22, 23, 25, 26, 28, 29, 31, 37, 41, 43, 45, 46, 49, 51, 55, 56, 58, 61, 64, 67, 72, 77, 82, 85, 86, 97, 100, 101, 103, 106, 111, 113, 114, 119, 127, 130, 137, 144—monsters © mers1na/Shutterstock.com
p.14—question marks © Nikolaeva/Shutterstock.com, scribble © MagicDogWorkshop/Shutterstock.com
p.22—emojis © browndogstudios/Shutterstock.com
p.23—sabre-toothed tiger © DIGITALIDAD/Shutterstock.com
p.25—park © advent/Shutterstock.com
p.28—doodles in thought bubbles © Daniela Barreto/Shutterstock.com
p.31—boy and germs © advent/Shutterstock.com
p.32—ghost and girl in bed © advent/Shutterstock.com
p.37—flipchart easel © advent/Shutterstock.com
pp.38 and 39—brains © Katrina Lee/Shutterstock.com
p.44—hand © Panda Vector/Shutterstock.com
pp.46–48—speech bubbles © mhatzapa/Shutterstock.com

CREDITS

Shutterstock.com, palette and paintbrush © Khabarushka/Shutterstock.com
p.130—children © advent/Shutterstock.com
p.131—thought bubble © NastyaBob/Shutterstock.com
p.132—question marks © Nikolaeva/Shutterstock.com
p.133—spa items © Daniela Barreto/Shutterstock.com